C000116703

Published by
Books By Boxer, Leeds, LS13 4BS UK
Books by Boxer (EU), Dublin D02 P593 IRELAND
© Books By Boxer 2021
All Rights Reserved
MADE IN MALTA

ISBN: 9781909732858

IT IS ILLEGAL FOR A PLAYER
TO RUB ANY SUBSTANCE OTHER
THAN SALVIA OR SWEAT ONTO
THE BALL, AS TAMPERING IN
CRICKET IS COMMON TO ACHIEVE
MORE FAVOURABLE BOWLING
CONDITIONS. WHEN BALL
TAMPERING, PLAYERS WOULD USE
LIP BALM OR OTHER GREASY
SUBSTANCES TO SMOOTH
OUT ONE SIDE OF THE BALL,
MAKING IT PASS EASIER THROUGH
THE AIR.

Law 42.5:
Any member of the fielding side may polish the ball providing that such polishing wastes no time and no artificial substance is used. No one shall rub the ball on the ground or use any artificial substance or take any other action to alter the condition of the ball.

THE FIRST WOMEN'S CRICKET
WORLD CUP WAS HELD IN 1973
AND WAS PLAYED TWO YEARS
BEFORE THE MEN'S WORLD
CUP IN 1975. THE ENGLAND
TEAM WON.

Women's cricket can be traced all the way back to the 1700's, with the first match being played in 1745.

LESLIE HYLTON OF WEST INDIES
IS THE ONLY CRICKETER TO BE
HANGED FOR MURDER. HE WAS
CONVICTED OF MURDERING
HIS WIFE, LURINE ROSE,
WHOM HE HAD SHOT 7 TIMES
IN A JEALOUS RAGE IN 1954.

Leslie Hylton.

- Born 29 March 1905 - Died 17 May 1955
- **Batting:** Right-handed
- **Bowling:** Right-arm fast

THE LONGEST EVER CRICKET MATCH
WAS PLAYED IN 1939 BETWEEN
ENGLAND AND SOUTH AFRICA
LASTING FOR 12 DAYS!

BEGINNING ON FRIDAY 3RD
MARCH, IT CONTINUED FOR
43 HOURS AND 16 MINUTES.

The game was declared a draw before
it was finished as the English team had to leave
for their ship to take them back home.

THE ONLY RULE TO NOT HAVE BEEN CHANGED FROM THE LAWS OF THE GAME (FIRST WRITTEN IN 1774 BY THE MCC), IS THAT THE LENGTH OF THE PITCH SHOULD BE 22 YARDS, OR 61.31 SQUARE METRES.

Law 6.1

The pitch is a rectangular area of the ground 22 yards/20.12 m in length and 10 ft./3.05 m in width. It is bounded at either end by the bowling creases and on either side by imaginary lines, one each side of the imaginary line joining the centres of the two middle stumps, each parallel to it and 5 ft./1.52 m from it.

THERE USED TO ONLY BE 2 STUMPS
ON A WICKET. THE THIRD STUMP
WAS INTRODUCED IN 1775, AFTER
CRICKETER LUMPY STEVENS
BOWLED THREE CONSECUTIVE
DELIVERIES THAT WENT
STRAIGHT THROUGH THE TWO
STUMPS WITHOUT HITTING THEM.

Edward 'Lumpy' Stevens
- **Born:** 1735 (exact date unknown)
- **Died:** 7 September 1819 (aged 83–84)
- **Batting:** Right-handed
- **Bowling:** Right-arm medium-fast

Sunil Manohar Gavaskar was almost switched at birth! His uncle noticed that the baby was not in fact Sunil. He was found in another bed and both babies were returned to their rightful families. The family involved in the incident were fishers by trade.

Sunil 'Sunny' Gavaskar

- **Born**: 10th July 1949
- **Batting**: Right-handed
- **Bowling**: Right-arm medium
- Sunil was born with a small hole
  in his ear, which helped his uncle
  spot the swap. Sunil could very
  well have been a professional
  fisherman.

IN 1992, SACHIN TENDULKAR BECAME THE FIRST EVER CRICKETER TO BE DISMISSED BY A THIRD UMPIRE FOLLOWING A TELEVISION REPLAY IN A TEST MATCH. BEFORE THEN, TECHNOLOGY WASN'T USED TO MAKE DECISIONS IN-GAME.

Sachin Ramesh Tendulkar

- **Born:** 24th April 1973
- **Batting:** Right-handed
- **Bowling:** Right-arm medium, leg break, off break
- During his early days of cricket, Sachin once put a hose pipe into Sourav Ganguly's (Sachin's former teammate and captain) room and turned on the tap!

IN 2012, CHRIS GAYLE PLAYED WITH
THE WEST INDIES AGAINST
BANGLADESH IN A TEST MATCH.
CHRIS HIT A SIX OFF THE FIRST
BALL IN THE GAME – THE FIRST
PERSON TO DO SO IN 137 YEARS!

Christopher Henry Gayle

- **Born:** 21st September 1979
- **Batting:** Left-handed
- **Bowling:** Right-arm off break
- Chris had difficulties in his early cricketing career due to suffering from an irregular heartbeat. He had to undergo an operation as treatment.

DURING THE 1999 CRICKET WORLD CUP, THE SOUTH AFRICAN CAPTAIN AND HIS COACH WERE ASKED TO REMOVE EARPIECES THAT WERE SPOTTED ON TV. THE EARPIECES WERE USED BY THE COACH TO GIVE INSTRUCTIONS TO THE CAPTAIN. NO OTHER ACTION WAS TAKEN.

While not against the laws of the game, there are no provisions set in place for the use of communication devices and the International Cricket Council did not condone such actions. Hansie Cronje, pictured with the covered earpiece from the match in question.

Abbas Ali Baig was the first Indian cricketer to be kissed during a Test. At the Brabourne Stadium in 1960.

After scoring 50 runs against Australia, a female fan came into the grounds and began kissing him repeatedly.

Abbas Ali Baig

- **Born:** 19th March 1939
- **Batting:** Right-handed
- **Bowling:** Leg break
- Abbas has three younger brothers
  (Murtuza Baig, Mazhar Baig, and
  Mujtaba Baig) who all played professional cricket.

Not only has Ellyse Perry played in the FIFA Women's World Cup for Matildas (Australia), but she has previously played in the ICC 2009 Cricket World cup, and was also part of the winning team of the 2013 Cricket World Cup.

Ellyse Alexandra Perry
- **Born:** 3rd November 1990
- **Batting:** Right-handed
- **Bowling:** Right-arm fast
- Ellyse is the first Australian to represent her country in both the cricket and football world cups.

IN CRICKET LAW, IT IS ILLEGAL TO TAMPER WITH THE BALL IN WAYS SUCH AS:

RUBBING THE BALL ON THE GROUND.

SCRATCHING THE BALL WITH FINGERNAILS OR SHARP OBJECTS.

RUBBING SUBSTANCES ONTO THE BALL.

In 2018, during the third Test match against South Africa, an Australian player, along with his captain and vice-captain, were all found to be tampering with the cricket ball and were made to step down for a full year.

THE FIRST EVER DOUBLE CENTURY
IN THE ONE DAY INTERNATIONAL
IS HELD BY AUSTRALIAN
BATSWOMAN BELINDA CLARK,
WHO HIT 229 RUNS AGAINST
DENMARK IN THE 1997 WOMEN'S
WORLD CUP.

Belinda Jane Clark
- **Born:** 10th September 1970
- **Batting:** Right-handed
- **Bowling:** Right-arm offbreak
- In 2011, Belinda was inducted in the International Cricket Council Hall of Fame.

IN 2006, JASON GILLESPIE SCORED 201 (NOT OUT), THE ONLY DOUBLE CENTURY SCORED BY A NIGHT WATCHMAN. FURTHER TO THIS, JASON SCORED THIS ON HIS FINAL INTERNATIONAL CRICKET MATCH!

Jason Neil Gillespie
- **Born:** 19th April 1975
- **Batting:** Right-handed
- **Bowling:** Right-arm fast
- Jason is vegan and doesn't approve of dairy farming or the use of leather in cricket balls.

ONE OF THE FIRST RECORDED
CRICKET GAMES WAS PLAYED IN
1646. LATER IN THE 1600'S, FINES
WERE HANDED OUT TO THOSE
WHO MISSED CHURCH TO PLAY.

Churches in the 1600's rarely condoned playing sports, especially cricket as this was a sport often played on Sundays.

DURING A TOUR OF ZIMBABWE IN
1984, BATSMAN GREG RITCHIE
WAS HELD FROM PLAYING
DUE TO AN ILLNESS. WHILE
HIS TEAM WERE PLAYING, HE LET
CHIMPANZEES LOSE IN THEIR
LOCKER ROOM!

Gregory Michael Ritchie

- **Born:** 23rd January 1960
- **Batting:** Right-handed
- **Bowling:** Right-arm medium
- After his cricketing career, Greg became an after-dinner speaker, travel agent, and starred on some sporting TV and radio shows.

Alec Stewart was born on the 8th April 1963. By the time he retired, he had scored a grand 8463 Test runs, matching his birthday – Talk about coincidence!

Alec James Stewart
- **Born:** 8/4/63 (scored 8463 Test runs)
- **Batting:** Right-handed
- **Bowling:** Right-arm medium
- An avid supporter of Chelsea F.C, when Alec had to pick a shirt number, he picked number 4 in honour of his favourite Chelsea player, John Hollins.

IN 1930, WILFRED RHODES MADE HIS
58TH AND FINAL APPEARANCE
IN AN INTERNATIONAL CRICKET
GAME, AT AGE 52 YEARS AND
165 DAYS OLD, WILFRED IS
THE OLDEST PLAYER TO HAVE
APPEARED IN A TEST MATCH!

Wilfred Rhodes
- **Born:** 29th October 1877
- **Died:** 8th July 1973 (aged 95)
- **Batting:** Right-handed
- **Bowling:** Slow left-arm orthodox
- By 1952, Wilfred was completely blind but still regularly attended cricket matches and followed the game with his hearing.

IN THE 2015 ICC WORLD CUP,
KUMAR SANGAKKARA BECAME
THE FIRST CRICKETER IN THE
WORLD TO SCORE 4 SUCCESSIVE
CENTURIES. THE RUNS WERE
AGAINST BANGLADESH,
ENGLAND, AUSTRALIA
AND SCOTLAND.

Kumar Chokshanada Sangakkara

- **Born:** 27th October 1977
- **Batting:** Left-handed
- **Bowling:** Right-arm off break

When Kumar was just 6 years old, his parents helped to shelter Tamil families during the Black July riots in 1983.

THE ONLY CRICKETER ON RECORD
TO HAVE PLAYED TEST CRICKET
FOR BOTH INDIA AND ENGLAND
IS IFTIKHAR ALI KHAN PATAUDI,
INDIAN ACTOR SAIF ALI KAHN'S
GRANDFATHER!

Iftikhar Ali Khan Pataudi
- **Born:** 16th March 1910
- **Died:** 5th January 1952 (aged 41)
- **Batting:** Right-handed

Iftikhar held the royal title 'Nawab of Pataudi', which is a family lineage of rulers in Northern India. The title was abolished in 1971.

CRICKET WAS THE FIRST 'BAT AND BALL' GAME PLAYED IN THE US AND BECAME INCREASINGLY POPULAR BETWEEN 1834-1914 ACROSS 46 STATES. THE POPULAR US SPORT BASEBALL HAS MANY CHARACTERISTICS THAT CAN BE FOUND IN EARLY BRITISH CRICKET GAMES.

The first reporting of a cricket match in America was in 1751, When a New York newspaper wrote an article about a game between New York and London.

NEIL McKENZIE IS POSSIBLY THE
WORLD'S MOST SUPERSTITIOUS
BATSMAN. NEIL HAD A NUMBER
OF STRANGE SUPERSTITIONS
THAT HE FOLLOWED.

HE FEARED STEPPING ON WHITE
LINES, TAPED HIS BAT TO THE
CEILING THE NIGHT BEFORE A
MATCH AND WOULD ENSURE THE
TOILET SEATS WERE DOWN AND
ALL OF THE CHANGING ROOM
LIGHTS WERE OFF BEFORE GOING
OUT TO BAT.

Neil McKenzie
- **Born:** 24 November 1975
- **Batting:** Right-handed
- **Bowling:** Right-arm medium
- Announced retirement from all forms of cricket in January 2016.

FREDERICK, PRINCE OF WALES DIED IN 1751 AFTER COMPLICATIONS OF BEING HIT BY A CRICKET BALL. FREDERICK WAS A CRICKET ENTHUSIAST, EVENTUALLY PLAYING AS A COUNTY CRICKETER FOR SURREY. HIS DEATH WAS PREVIOUSLY THOUGHT TO BE A BURST LUNG ABSCESS, BUT IS NOW THOUGHT TO HAVE BEEN A BLOCKAGE IN HIS LUNG CAUSED BY THE BLOW FROM A CRICKET BALL.

- Frederick, Prince of Wales
- **Born:** 31 January 1707
- **Died:** 31 March 1751 (Aged 44)
- **Cause of Death:** Cricket Ball

IN ENGLAND, 8-BALL OVERS WERE ADOPTED BRIEFLY IN 1939, WITH AN INTENTION TO CARRY THIS ON IN 1940. HOWEVER, DUE TO THE SECOND WORLD WAR, INTERNATIONAL CRICKET HAD BEEN HELD AND FOLLOWING THIS, ENGLAND REVERTED BACK TO 6-BALL OVERS.

The only country which cricket was not disrupted by the Second World War was India, which was able to keep their normal schedule of matches throughout.

W.G. GRACE WAS THE FIRST
CRICKETER TO PUBLICLY SUPPORT
A PRODUCT. IN 1895 HE BECAME AN
AMBASSADOR FOR
COLMAN'S MUSTARD.

WITH THE TAGLINE
'COLMAN'S MUSTARD
HEADS THE FIELD'
YOU CAN STILL BUY HIS MUSTARD
MERCHANDISE TODAY!

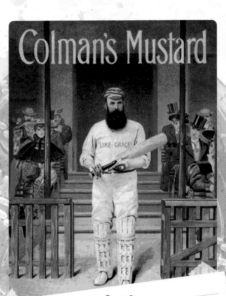

William Gilbert Grace
- **Born:** 18th July 1848
- **Died:** 23rd October 1915
- **Batting:** Right-handed
- **Bowling:** Right-arm medium
- W.G. Grace's height was a massive 6ft, 2in, which is substantially taller than the average male in the 1800's.

THE FIRST GROUND IN ENGLAND
TO HOLD A TEST MATCH WASN'T
THE FAMOUS LORD'S CRICKET
GROUND, BUT RATHER THE
OVAL CRICKET GROUND. IN
1880, IT BECAME THE VENUE
FOR ENGLAND'S FIRST EVER
TEST MATCH AGAINST AUSTRALIA.

The Oval Cricket Ground was the
second ground to ever stage a Test, after
Melbourne Cricket Ground in Australia.

THE WORD CRICKET HAS BEEN
USED FOR THE INSECT FOR MUCH
LONGER THAN THE SPORTS. THE
INSECT HAS HAD IT'S NAME SINCE
AT LEAST 1325, THOUGH THE
FIRST RECORDED USE FOR THE
SPORT WAS IN 1575.

The cricket insect was named simply
for the noises it makes, though the sport
was named after an old French word
meaning 'goal post'.

DENIS COMPTON NOT ONLY WAS A
BATSMAN FOR ENGLAND BUT HE
ALSO PLAYED FOOTBALL FOR ARSENAL

AT ARSENAL HE SCORED 15 GOALS
IN HIS CAREER, NOTABLY WINNING
THE LEAGUE TITLE IN 1948 AND
THE FA CUP IN 1950. WHILST
COMPTON FINISHED HIS CRICKET
CAREER AFTER PLAYING 78 TEST
MATCHES WITH 17 CENTURIES,
IN ALL FIRST-CLASS CRICKET HE
SCORED 123 CENTURIES.

Football Team
- **Team:** Arsenal: 1936-1950
- **Position:** Winger

Cricket Team
- **Team:** Middlesex: 1936-1958
- **Batting:** Right-handed
- **Bowling:** Left-arm unorthodox spin

THE WEIGHT AND SIZE OF A CRICKET BALL IS VERY IMPORTANT WHEN PLAYING, AS DIFFERENT SIZES AND WEIGHTS COULD GIVE PLAYERS AN ADVANTAGE SUCH AS ALLOWING A BALL TO GO FASTER. THERE IS EVEN A CRICKET LAW THAT STATES WHAT SIZES ARE ACCEPTABLE.

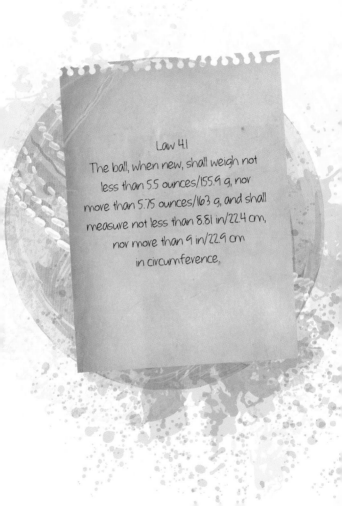

Law 4.1
The ball, when new, shall weigh not
less than 5.5 ounces/155.9 g, nor
more than 5.75 ounces/163 g, and shall
measure not less than 8.81 in/22.4 cm,
nor more than 9 in/22.9 cm
in circumference.

Before playing in the 1983 World Cup and beating the West Indies team by 43 runs, India had only defeated one other cricket team, which was East Africa.

In 2011, India became the first cricket team to win the World Cup while also hosting the final match.

Inzamam-ul-Haq is a Pakistani cricketer who not only took a wicket on the very first ball of his international bowling career, but the person he sent back to the dressing room was

Brian Lara

who is widely acknowledged as one of the greatest batsman of all time and a member of the ICC's hall of fame, inducted in January 2012. Inzamam-ul-Haq took a wicket for 45 at the Iqbal Stadium, Faisalabad in 1991.

Inzamam-ul-Haq:

- Captain of the Pakistan National Cricket team from 2003–7.
- **Nickname:** Inzi
- **Batting:** Right-handed
- **Bowling:** Slow left-arm orthodox

IN THE FIRST EVER TEST IN 1877, AUSTRALIA BEAT ENGLAND BY 45 RUNS.

100 YEARS LATER IN THE CENTENARY TEST, AUSTRALIA BEAT ENGLAND AGAIN WITH 45 RUNS – THE EXACT SAME!

Commerative Stamps from
the centenary test match.

A CRICKET SCORE CALLED A 'NELSON' IS SAID TO BE BAD LUCK. THE SCORE, BEING 111, IS SAID TO RESEMBLE THREE STUMPS WITHOUT BAILS, AND WILL CAUSE UNLUCKY AND BAD THINGS TO HAPPEN TO THE PLAYER AND THEIR TEAM.

The late David Shepherd (Umpire),
used to stand on one leg when
a Nelson was scored in an attempt to
counter the supposed superstition.

NEWLY PURCHASED CRICKET BATS
SHOULD BE TREATED BY
RUBBING IT DOWN WITH
LINSEED OIL, AN OIL THAT
FILLS IN THE GRAINS IN
WOOD, LEAVING THE BAT
WITH A TOUGHER HITTING
SURFACE WHICH WILL REDUCE
CRACKS AND SPLINTERS OVER TIME.

Linseed is the only oil you can use on a cricket bat safely. All other oils will damage cricket bats over time.

AFTER BEATING THE WEST INDIES BY 351 RUNS, ALL 11 PLAYERS IN THE SOUTH AFRICA TEAM SHARED THE MAN OF THE MATCH AWARD, AS THEY ALL CONTRIBUTED EQUALLY IN THEIR VICTORY.

There has been many
instances in cricket where a member
of the losing team has been
awarded man of the match,
due to contributing to the game.

Brendan Taylor (Zimbabwe's wicket-keeper batsman) was paid an insignificant 250 USD for the entire 2015 World Cup. This was due to Zimbabwe not having the funds to pay extra.

Brendan Taylor

Other countries such as Australia
paid each player around 5000 USD each.

THE SHORTEST TEST MATCH WAS
BETWEEN WEST INDIES AND
ENGLAND IN THE 2009 TEST
SERIES AND LASTED ONLY 10
BALLS BEFORE IT WAS CALLED
OFF DUE TO BOWLERS UNABLE
TO GET A SOLID FOOTING.

The shortest completed test match was between England and Australia held at the Trent bridge Stadium in June 1926, resulting in a draw with just 50 minutes play and 17.2 overs bowled.

STEVE WAUGH CARRIED A RED
RAG WITH HIM IN HIS POCKET
EVERY TIME HE TOOK TO THE
CRICKET FIELD. HE WAVED HE
RAG TO THE CROWD AS HIS
LEFT THE FIELD ON HIS 168TH
AND FINAL TEST MATCH IN SYDNEY.

THIS WAS INDIA'S TOUR OF
AUSTRALIA, 4TH TEST, JAN 2 -
6TH 2004. 4-MATCH SERIES
DRAWN 1-1

Steve Waugh.
Australian Captain from 1997-2004, he is considered to be
one of the most successful Test captains in history, with
41 victories. He was awarded the Australian of the Year
award in 2004, for his cricketing feats as well as
for his work with charities.

ONE CRICKET BALL ONCE
TRAVELLED 556 MILES! JIMMY
SINCLAIR WAS BATTING AT
THE OLD WANDERERS
STADIUM IN JOHANNESBURG.
THE STADIUM BORDERS A
TRAIN TRACK AND AFTER A HIT
FROM SINCLAIR THE BALL FLEW
OUT OF THE GROUND AND
LANDED ON A TRAIN ON IT'S
WAY TO PORT ELIZABETH.

Jimmy Sinclair.

Jimmy Sinclair was the first cricketer from any country to score
both a century and take five wickets in an innings
in the same Test. He notably scored South
Africa's first three test centuries and is known as one
of the fastet scoring Test batsmen.

THE CRICKET PLAYER WITH THE
LONGEST NAME IS FIJI'S IL BULA –
HIS FULL NAME IS ILIKENA
LASARUSA TALEBULAMAINAVALEN-
IVEIVAKABULAIMAINAKULALAKE-
IBALAU. WHICH TRANSLATES TO
RETURNED ALIVE FROM NANKULA
HOSPITAL AT LAKEBA ISLAND IN
THE LAU GROUP.

I.L Bula
- **Batting:** Right-handed
- I.L. was posthumously inducted into Fiji Sports Hall of Fame in September 2005.
- **Last First-class:** 12 January 1956 Fiji v West Indians
- **First-class debut:** 13 February, 1948 Fiji v Auckland

SOUTH AFRICA DID NOT LOSE A
SINGLE TEST SERIES AWAY FROM
HOME BETWEEN 2006 AND
2015. AFTER 9 WHOLE YEARS OF
NOT LOSING A SINGLE GAME,
INDIA FINALLY BEAT
THEM BY 124 RUNS.

South Africa holds the record for the
second longest unbeaten streak in away series
Test cricket. West Indies hold the lead with
16 years being unbeaten.

A CRICKET GAME WAS ONCE STOPPED BECAUSE A PIG RAN ACROSS THE FIELD. AFTER PUTTING AN APPLE IN THE PIGS MOUTH, AN UNKNOWN MAN CONVINCED GUARDS THAT THE PIG WOULD BE HIS LUNCH. THE PIG WAS EVENTUALLY RELEASED ONTO THE PITCH WITH 'EDDIE' WRITTEN ON ONE SIDE AND 'BEEFY' ON THE OTHER.

It is legal to suspend the game if
any animal enters the field in which a game
of cricket is being played.

THE YOUNGEST INTERNATIONAL
CRICKET PLAYER IN HISTORY
WAS PAKISTANI PLAYER
HASAN RAZA, WHO WAS
AGED JUST 14 YEARS AND
227 DAYS WHEN HE
FIRST REPRESENTED HIS
COUNTRY IN 1996.

Hasan Raza

- **Team:** Pakistan (1996-2005)
- **Caps:** 140 (**Test**) and 110 (**ODI**)
- **Dates active:** 1996-2018
- **Batting:** Right-Handed
- **Bowling:** Right arm off break.

ON 11TH NOVEMBER 2011 (11/11/11),
AT 11.11AM, SOUTH AFRICA
NEEDED 111 RUNS TO WIN THE
FIRST TEST MATCH AGAINST
AUSTRALIA.

AS THE SCOREBOARD READ: 11.11 11/11/
SPECTATORS AND THE UMPIRE
IAN GOULD STOOD ON ONE LEG
IN REFERENCE TO DAVID SHEPHERD'
TRADITION OF RAISING A LEG
FROM THE GROUND ON NELSON
TO AVOID BAD LUCK.

Score board from Newlands
Cricket Stadium, Cape Town, South Africa.

MOST CRICKET BATS IN ENGLAND
ARE MADE FROM WILLOW
DUE TO IT BEING LIGHTWEIGHT,
TOUGH AND SHOCK-RESISTANT.
WHITE WILLOW HAS BECOME
WELL KNOWN AS CRICKET
BAT WILLOW.

Most bats can't be used straight away
after purchasing, as they require
'knocking-in' to stop the bat from
being damaged when hitting a ball.

SIR VIVIAN RICHARDS, KNIGHTED
FOR HIS CONTRIBUTION TO
CRICKET, NOT ONLY PLAYED
IN THE CRICKET WORLD CUP
IN 1975 AND 1979 FOR THE WEST
INDIES BUT ALSO HAS PLAYED IN
THE FOOTBALL WORLD CUP
QUALIFYING MATCHES FOR
ANTIGUA IN 1974.

Sir Vivian Richards

- **Team:** West Indies (1974-1991)
- **Caps:** 151 (**Test**) and 14 (**ODI**)
- **Dates active:** 1974-1991
- **Nickname:** Master Blaster, King Viv